M.

www.saintsriot.com

ISBN-10: 0692597131
ISBN-13: 978-0692597132

Hey there, handsome.

Before you say another word,
please remember that I am not yours.

I remember when we were sweet. We walked Vegas like kids playing Cowboy in our fathers' shoes. I'd never been so far away from home.

You said that my eyes lit up when the fountains shot into the air.

Do they still light up? Do my eyes still light up at things?

He stains like a pomegranate.
I keep thinking about the way
his toes moved in the water.

The night that you killed me,
the last thought I had was:
But I'm getting blood on his shoes.

I wonder what the kisses in Brooklyn taste like. In my head, there's a brown-eyed Love Jones in a pair of sick red Adidas who's calling up to my window at one A.M. He wants to take me out into the night with a thermos full of Sangria, and he's threatening to wake my neighbors up by singing cock rock at the top of his lungs until I say yes. Later, with our lips stained red and our feet in a park fountain's water, he's the one who shows me.

Roy Boy blow the horn and he in town. Every year, sure as a clock. Them boys be callin' but I keeps my head down.

He say I'm his favorite. The way his lips curl 'round that pipe. How wild his face look.

After the show, I'll fry him my buttermilk chicken. I'll light a stick o' incense by the window and rub a worry or two out his shoulders. Then I'll turn my blanket down and let him in. He hold my hips like he hold that pipe.

He be gone by daybreak, but that don't bother me none. He be back. He say I'm his favorite. Them boys be callin' but I keeps my head down.

❦.

where we can blow the confetti
off of each other's lips.

I held him the night that he drove his fist into my face. Took his head right into my lap. He curled his knees into my hip, brought my waist into his arms. His tears left a stain on my jeans, but I didn't mind much. I held him. Because we both knew that it would be the last time I'd ever.

I hungered for an apple, so you gifted me an orange grove, as oranges are your favorite fruit. Now, despite my professions of gratitude, you wonder why I never smile when you pull my chair out to eat.

●

Don't kiss me if you need eight hours to dream at night. I'm not the kind of lover who will leave you committed to your sleep.

he's sweet and he's kind and he texts you all day long and he's totally good with kids and he kisses away his grudges and he gets along with all of your friends and he knows when to put the drink down and he's a great cook and he never uses foul language and he wants to hold you after you come and he knows how to sit still when you have your boss over for dinner and he loves all of the foods that you love and he loves all of the movies that you love and he's into all of the bands that you're into and of course he'll go to dinner with you and your rude friend jenny and he dyes his hair the same shade as yours and he wears contacts colored the same as your eyes and sometimes you wake in the middle of the night to find him standing over you and he mimics the way that you laugh and he mimics the way that you walk and he gets his name changed to yours and he starts calling your mom in your voice because she can no longer tell the difference and you realize that you're dating yourself and it's kind of creepy, and that's when you'll miss me.

❧

If you'd like me to wait for you
because you love me most,
I'm begging you to tell me now

before he gets too close.

Our mouths were full of butterflies once again, so we were just going to let it pass. And then, miles away, a truck hit a power pole and the lights went out in the county. We looked above us and the sky was a sheet of stars. We could barely see each other, but your hands found my face and you pulled me into a kiss. Every word we'd been wanting to say we left right there on the other's lips.

❧

I can take your yellow shirt. While you wear it. Hook my fingers into the collar. Lift the bottom to meet it. Take your skin between my teeth. Leave a little bruise. I like your yellow shirt.

I can take your V-neck. Roll it in my hands until it's rope. Lay you down. Bind your wrists together with it. Lift them over your head. Lock them behind your neck. I like your V-neck.

I can take your blue shirt. Grip the top in one hand and the bottom in the other. Raise it above your head and around your neck. Bring you close. Lower it down your back. Take you by the waist. Bring our bodies together. I like your blue shirt.

I can take your flannel. Tie its sleeves around your naked waist. That should give me something to hold on to.

I can take your tank. Take it straight from your bedroom floor. Wear it all day long. See you in every fold, every wrinkle. Hear you in every brush of the pulled cotton. Wear you on my skin. I like your tank.

♦

He is beautiful. Skin as copper. Hair as a raven's wing. Tall and strong.

Yes, God, he is beautiful.

But when he falls asleep, I'm going to put my clothes back on and go home.

I came to the city with two shirts, three-hundred dollars and my brother's old backpack. I was deer-eyes then. The chrome and the lights. It was all so pretty. I would have went with anyone. But he found me. Plucked me like a tulip from a patch. He saw me crystal in a city, gray. My lover and my only friend between the concrete and the faces.

I love him. I love him so.

But when he falls asleep, I'm going to put my clothes back on and go home.

I took rain on my face for the first time in months today. The storm was over as soon as it began (it doesn't rain here like it does back home), but I'd forgotten about rain, and apple trees, and skies that go on and on and on.

The faces in this city, they're so closed, so bitter. I saw a man spit on a homeless woman once. Spit right in her face. Nobody did a thing. I didn't do a thing. Back home, I would have done something. Back home, a man would never spit on a woman. *Why didn't I do anything?* I've become so closed, so bitter. I can't be so closed, so bitter.

But he loves the city. The city speaks to him in languages that I can't understand. He'd never leave. Not even for me. I love him too much to ask him to.

I can't go on without feeling rain. *Real* rain. Or hearing kind words, or walking dirt roads in the shade of apple trees. I can't stay.

I've got some money saved up from the diner. Enough for a bus ticket. Mama's expecting me in two days time. This will be a sting too great to think twice about. If we'd just met somewhere else. Maybe beneath an apple tree. Maybe in the rain.

He hasn't put his arm around me tonight. I'm grateful for that. I listen to him next to me. Shallow breaths. Not quite there yet. I need his eyes closed. I need his mind at peace. I need him asleep.

Almost there, almost there.

Sleep.

Sleep, and dream about new lovers between the concrete and the fog.

He is beautiful.

But when he falls asleep, I'm going to put my clothes back on and go home.

·⠂●●

and then there's sunday when i want you here in the back of the laundromat while our darks tumble dry.

To the men who have
loved on my body,

its curves and its twists

its softs and its roughs

its smooths and its thicks

its cuts and its bends,

you all suck.

We used to have a lot of fun.

By we, I mean you.

By fun, I mean nerve.

I know that I should wish for money. I should wish for superpowers or world peace. But, if I only get one, I wish that he'd let me run my fingers through his curls. Just once.

᛫ᛈ

Two years ago, I wasn't the same.
Two years from now should worry you.

adr i f   t...

Beware your tongue, my love.
You may curse me like the scorned,
but I can curse you like a witch.

you've forgotten
what it was like
down

here
with

me.

Those lips. That kiss, man. I don't know what I'm going to do with you.

dis
connect
your
self from me.
you are
far
too hea
vy.

Don't ask me again what I'd do
when you know very well that I'd go.

Loving myself
feels an awful lot
like hating you.

Hating myself
feels an awful lot
like loving you.

He's beautiful, isn't he?

That was taken in France.

I hate mountain hiking, actually. I'm scared of heights. I wanted to go shopping that day. But Mateo said that I needed the fresh air. Halfway up, I went vertigo, stumbled and twisted my ankle. Mateo made it to the very top.

You should hear the words that come out of Mateo's wonderful mouth. He wanted to be a lawyer once. He never lets me win a case.

Mateo doesn't like it when I leave the table from his dinner parties, even if it's just to use the restroom.

I make him laugh.

Mateo knows how to dress. The man always looks like a million bucks. He's even helped me with my style. "No man of mine will wear a T-shirt," he says. Now I have all of these button-ups in blues and tangerines. Mateo tells me they look great with my skin tone.

Mateo takes me to the symphony. He doesn't like rock and roll so much. He doesn't like it when I blast my music. "Just below your speaking voice," he says. "That's where music should be."

Mateo is so charming. Mateo doesn't want me opening my own car door. Mateo bought me dye when he found a gray hair on my head. Mateo's so attentive. Mateo doesn't like for me to smoke. Mateo hates it when I drink.

Mateo will only buy veggies for the house. "I want to keep you healthy and fit," he says. Mateo looks out for me. Mateo cares.

Mateo loves his friends. He has this friend, Miguel. They work together. Miguel is very handsome with his dark eyes and his salt-and-pepper hair. Mateo and Miguel are two peas in a pod. Mateo and Miguel do Boys Nights in Vegas. Miguel works in and out of town. He's always moving around, so Mateo helps him with his stuff. Mateo spends a lot of time with Miguel.

In fact, that's where he is now. Helping Miguel move once again. Left out of here in his favorite T-shirt without saying a word. He texted and told me they'd be stopping for burgers and drinks afterwards.

And here I am with Mateo's symphony and Mateo's hair dye and Mateo's veggies and Mateo's button-ups, and a picture of his smile on a mountain in France.

So you see, you don't have to worry about Mateo. Not tonight.

Pass me my drink, please.

Pass me my drink, take your clothes off and turn the volume on the record player all the way up.

●.

My skin is swollen with your revolutions. I keep combing your rebellions out of my hair. Maybe if I told you about the war between my throat and my belly, you'd stick around long enough to choose a side in it.

That was love I braided against your scalp last Tuesday. That was love with stained fingers from the paint of your picket signs. You save the thirsty and the dying, but both share your bed.

I make you sandwiches you'll forget to thank me for on your way out to another protest. I take milk and hoses to your stinging eyes. I pass large bowls of rice and squash out to your weary soldiers.

I'm dynamite every time the phone rings and you're gone. How can you save a world when you can't see the one right in front of you? My voice might not stretch as far as yours does, my dude, but I'm the only one calling your name.

My cigarette might be killing me,
but better it than you.

Someth ng's m ss ng between us.

I fell for a man who fell for a woman who stunk of weed and hated me so. How could he prefer her kisses over mine? My tongue tastes of guava fruit.

When you say that you love someone, you're to wear them as a crown. So why am I here by a string on your wrist? Why do you hide me in your pocket when others are around? You take me off before you shower. You've lost me a few times between your sofa cushions. You say that you love me, but what is it like from the top of your head?

He will never change.
He will never change.
He will never change.
He will never change.
He will never change.
He will never change.
He will never change.
He will never change.

There is nothing I'd rather do
than to pretend like I can't dance
to dance with you.

I'm going to write him a love song. I'm going to sing it for him at the top of my lungs and it's going to call the cartoon birds down from the cartoon clouds.

Butterflies will land on our shoulders. Fawns will rest at our feet. Gazelles will rest their heads on the shoulders of lions. Babies all around the world will stop bawling and listen to the strange and pretty lullaby that's been thrown into the air. Soldiers at odds will drop their weapons and make out with one another right there on the battlefield. It's going to make the world fall in love with him. They'll sing along with me. A chorus of lovers. All for him.

I'm going to write him a love song.

And I hope that the wind carries it to your ears while you're kissing him, and it breaks your fucking heart.

I've asked these candles and this bottle of sandalwood oil. We can't figure out why you still have your belt fastened.

I died chewing gum
in my favorite T-shirt
with my hands in my pockets,
my boots in the dirt,
while the wind made my cheeks numb
and all the trees swayed
on that cold winter's night
when your car drove away.

My tongue in your ear, my hand in your jeans, and your feet were bare, so I had to stay careful not to step on your toes. I could have lowered your pants so that we didn't get them sticky, but I wasn't feeling particularly polite.

Four fingers and a thumb near the top. You were as hot as fevers in my hand. I took your chin into my mouth. You hit the wall behind me with the side of your fist. I went to your neck, lips open, tongue spelling a secret.

That was it for you.

You threw your chest into mine, screamed out a word that doesn't exist, and your hips bucked forward. Once. Twice.

Warmness. Between my fist and your boxers.
It fell onto my knuckles, between my fingers.

I had to wash my hands. You had to get to work. Neither of us moved a muscle. Both of us breathing hard, both of our hearts still racing.

❧.

We love the same poets
and we fit the same shoes,
but that's where our similarities end.
Me, and the man who would wait.

Between the tacos and the letters,
I thought you'd last forever.

My mouth's a Ferris wheel
when he's on the mind.

You care too much for others' thoughts
and far less for your lover's thoughts.
Until you, Sir, give this some thought,
we won't meet at the dance.

And in the barn, I'll swing alone.
I'll Allemande and Do-si-do.
Then, I will find my own way home.
We won't meet at the dance.

I don't know where he is now,
but I still sing for him.

Aliens have attacked and zombies are out for our brains. So *now* can you love me, sugar? *Now* can you be mine?

Dogs
Before
Boys.

"Then, why are you here?"

"Who said I was here?"

He never asks why I feel safer when I ride in the backseat. He only asks for me to lay my wrist on his shoulder from behind, so that he can kiss it at the stoplights.

If Billy can deliver 6 newspapers in 2 hours and Susie can deliver 20 newspapers in 8 hours, what do you think I mean when I say that I won't be looking back or taking you with me?

❦.

That is to say, you'll probably never see me again. And if you do, I'll probably never see you the same.

Trade shirts with you in the middle of a concert.

Take your hand and run with you through a
crowd like in a movie.

Drink ourselves silly-shit on the football field of
some high school we never went to.

Throw our own little parking lot prom.

We smell like cigarettes and gas station cologne.

We buy motorcycle goggles just for the hell of it
and wear 'em to the beach.

You put your fingers in my side just as the zombie
jumps out at us in the haunted house. I scream
like a woman. We laugh about it for the rest of
the Summer.

I like you on the kitchen table. If only the damn
dog would quit tugging at my socks.

You let me sleep there on your lap with the car
door open.

You make your erection dance in your jeans on purpose while we're sitting where I can't laugh out loud.

Children's Halloween masks and long days by the pool.

Fireworks and your hoodie around my shoulders.

Doing 90 with the sweating champagne bottle between my legs and your feet on the dashboard.

ink, star, planet,
star, star, planet,
venus, ink, star,
you.

If there are five personalities in the room,
but only you and he sitting there,
leave the room.

How many petals would you have me pick from these poor daisies? How many coins should hit the bottom of how many fountains? I light candles in reds and pinks, and every night, I turn in a new direction so that I don't wish on the same star twice.

❧

You gifted me white ribbons,
but neither of us saw them.

Dear M.,

I could have first fallen for those kind brown eyes or that wave of dark hair, but back then, you kept your face hidden beneath the shade of a fitted cap. So I settled for your hands. When you weren't watching me, I was watching your hands. I watched your knuckles tighten as they gripped your steering wheel. I studied the thick surface veins that snaked between them. Little ropes I imagined myself walking. You'd probably say that they were nothing special. To me, they were everything.

I've only ever felt them on my own hands in a handshake or around my shoulders in a friendly embrace. Every time, I wondered what they might feel like pressed into my lower back or warming my face on a cold night. I would have given anything for just one of those thumbs to brush a tear away from my cheek or to run itself across my lips.

I'd learn to love the rest of your parts as time went on, but if love was grown from seeds, your hands were my soil.

Tell me that you believe me.

Dear M.,

My daydreams of you were never, like, picnics by the river or slow dances at the prom.

I'd dream us on a road trip.

There was never any real destination, and the car changed every time I closed my eyes, but the set up was always the same: you, me, a radio on full blast, the open road and pockets full of beer money.

The romance would come in <u>how</u> we rode. Sometimes, you'd rest your hand over mine and we'd stay that way for miles. Sometimes, I'd rest my head in your lap. Sometimes...my head wouldn't be resting. (Once, I worked out an entire scenario where you had to climb into the backseat to meet me with your jeans bunched around your ankles.)

A sky full of stars or a noonday sun. Speeding. Slow. Goofy pictures at roadside diners. Tacky cowboy hats from middle-of-nowhere gas stations. Making out in front of truck drivers to drive them crazy. We'd roll the windows down and our clothes would whip like flags.

The ending was always the same, too.

Some cheap motel. We'd cling to each other so hard the sky wouldn't be able to tell where I ended and you began. My cheek on your collarbone. The backs of your fingers running along my earlobe.

You'd ask what I was thinking about.

"This."

"Nothing else?"

"Nothing else."

Tell me that you believe me.

Dear M.,

This isn't an unrequited love, it's a different kind of love. I know that I have a place with you and I know that I'll never feel your lips against mine.

And still, I'd give the last of my breath so that you could have one more. If you couldn't hear music, I'd give you my sound. If you couldn't kiss the one you loved, I'd give you my lips.

Even though it wouldn't be me.

If you were to find yourself with the ache that I feel for you now, I'd give you my words.

They're yours anyway.

The last time I saw you, you told me I hadn't changed, that I was still the same me you'd always known. I'm the same me you've never known too. The me who is mad for you.

Tell me that you believe me.

Dear M.,

Tes yeux, j'en rêve jour et nuit, and today, I love you like a French song.

I made this for you.

See?

Je suis amoureux.

Tell me that you believe me.

Dear M.,

If the sun
were to burn itself
completely out of the sky,
they'd find me beneath you,
the warmest thing in the world.

Tell me that you believe me.

Dear M.,

Your bandanna has twenty dollar bills drawn all over it. When you wrap it around your lower face, one of Andrew Jackson's heads rests right over your mouth.

My bandanna has cartoon bombs drawn all over it. When I wrap it around my lower face, a large one sits right over my mouth.

We kiss like this. Andrew and the Bomb. You, of freedom. Me, of passion. Red-blooded. Hot-hearted. They'll never see us coming.

We take the world on while we kiss the bruises from the other's cheek.

Tell me that you believe me.

Dear M.,

i wouldn't sleep on my wild,   if i were you.
   you think you've had crazy on you?

                              you've   never   had
crazy on you.   unzip
   your   pants and let me go crazy on
you.   i know you like your kisses sweet
   and your lovers sane,   but i bet i
   can make your heart   beat   like it's
   fighting   its way out of your chest.

                       i can make you hot.   a
kiss?   fuck a kiss.

        the only thing i'll   need to
kiss is your navel.   let me lay a
   little in your lap.   part your
knees,   i'll   make you grip your steering
wheel   with those beautiful hands   'til
your   knuckles go
white   like it's saving your life.   you
can keep   the sugar and spice   in the
jars.   i'm cinnamon   and sriracha.

                       i'm so not wound
tight up here.   let me   pull you
apart down there.   you know how i
don't stop talking   once i get going?   well.

        you   can   finally   shut   my   fucking
mouth,   or make me run it face down.

70

i never choke.   i never spit.
you'll ball your feet up like fists.
            i'm out of my fucking mind for you.
i wouldn't sleep on my   wild,   if i were
you.   they might   have   made
you moan.   i can make you scream.

Tell me you believe me.

Dear M.,

I think of you in blooms.
You start as a seed
somewhere between my nose and my crown. Then,
you sprout green.
You stretch into colors and petals,
winding and unfurling
until you're mapped across my head
and all I can see is you.

Also,
I've always wondered
what your erect penis looked like
and I hope one day that you'll show me.

Tell me that you believe me.

Pity you can't save me from these giants.
You look so cute in your coat and your tie.

●

You're never going back
to how you used to be,
are you?

◦

How did I die? I was crushed by the air of my own sigh the last time you asked me to wait just a little while longer.

❦

This is my poppet.
This is my spell.
Hope he felt good, motherfucker.

There is a blue ox, a dog with two heads, a jolly old man who delivers toys to children on Christmas Eve, and losing your favor is of great concern to me.

if my love was crowns,
your take be the throne.
if your love was steak,
my take be the bone.

Wait, so you're dragons? I've been calling you unicorns this entire time! Of *course* you're dragons! Why didn't you correct me?

❧

It's lovely, but I've got my own ballroom.

"The only reason that I put my shoes on is because you're really annoying and you wouldn't come."

Your love is in a very strange way.

Marvin's a cyclone. Marvin's a jerk. Marvin likes my trouble. Marvin has a goldfish tattooed on his arm. Marvin has the book that I was reading hidden behind his back. Marvin in his sweat pants. Marvin in his flip-flops. Marvin doesn't eat pork. Marvin doesn't like my best friend. Marvin won't kill a spider in the bathroom. Marvin won't sleep beneath the covers. Marvin believes in ghosts. Marvin believes in love. Marvin doesn't know you 'til he knows you. Marvin's an art activist who doesn't make art. Marvin likes his kisses dry. Marvin won't get out of bed. Marvin won't call his mother back. Marvin dreams of birds that drop grenades from their beaks and of making love to me in broad daylight right outside of a Sears department store. Marvin hates cheap beer. Marvin shares his popcorn. Marvin won't stop texting me. Marvin won't turn the music down. Marvin always runs hot. Marvin always dances while he's cooking. Marvin on the way to Vegas. Marvin on the way to save me. Marvin can be stubborn. Marvin can be sorry. Marvin cries. Marvin loves Jay-Z.

You and Me,
the bird and bee,
and as far away from where I need to be.

Our demons can't play together.

You rolled your jeans up over your calves and stood across from me in my bathwater. I thought that you were taking dirty pictures, but when you showed them to me, they were all of my face. You told me you liked the way I looked when my hair was wet.

Just me and you and bare feet and Chinese and 40s and A Nightmare on Elm Street and 40s and Chinese and feet bare and you and me Just me and you and bare feet and Chinese and 40s and A Nightmare on Elm Street and 40s and Chinese and feet bare and you and me Just me and you and bare feet and Chinese and 40s and A Nightmare on Elm Street and 40s and Chinese and feet bare and you and me Just me and you and bare feet and Chinese and 40s and A Nightmare on Elm Street and 40s and Chinese and feet bare and you and me Just me and you and bare feet and Chinese and 40s and A Nightmare on Elm Street and 40s and Chinese and feet bare and you and me Just me and you and bare feet and Chinese and 40s and A Nightmare on Elm Street and 40s and Chinese and feet bare and you and me Just me and you and bare feet and Chinese and 40s and A Nightmare on Elm Street and 40s and Chinese and feet bare and you and me Just me and you and bare feet and Chinese and 40s and

●

You threw the sheets away from your body and told me that I could watch. Eyes shut. Shorts pulled around your thighs. Your toes kept moving, but not in any particular rhythm. The only time I've ever loved being ignored.

While they were kicking my ass in that alleyway, I thought of us. They stomped on me like I was an aluminum can and all I could think about was how I'm your favorite boy. Now you're getting tears and snot and shit all over my hospital gown and my broken-bottle body. I get it. I'm a bruise and a stitch with at least the best of my teeth left. Baby, chill. You were there. Batman in the cologne that I love. Had me in your arms the entire time.

You weren't obsessed with Holden Caulfield, you were obsessed with Lennie Small. You told me that I was like Curley's Wife. I asked what you meant by that and you said, "You're so pretty, I could kill you."

Must have pretty eyes, pretty teeth, pretty skin, pretty hair, pretty fingernails, pretty genitals, a pretty mane, pretty scales, pretty organs, pretty wings, pretty pleases, pretty pretty princesses, pretty horns and a pretty tail.

Must have a good job, a nice apartment, a good credit score, a nice car, a good music collection, a nice three-headed dog, a good show pony, a nice baby grand piano, a good set of dragon-slaying swords, a nice set of bottle caps, a good collection of severed heads and a nice collection of falcons and owls.

Must have no children, no exes who are friends, no smoking habit, no bills, no love for his mother, no heart, no soul, no more, no problem, no bueno, no way, no personality, no imperfections, no goals, no dreams and no existence.

I am without boundaries.
I am not without standards.
If you want me to go down on you,
you have to take your socks off.

I just gave up drinking.
You're soon to go with it.
You'd best get that kiss
you've been planning on in.

To get there, just slide down the surface veins in his neck and make a left. Climb down the surface veins in his arms and keep going until you reach the surface veins in his ankle. Then, walk the surface veins in his foot (either one, any vein, they all lead to the same place), small leap from his toes and you've made it. Do you need me to write this down?

·♪

Hurry, before your boss

pastor

mother

catches us.

I'm stirring the roux for the gumbo
and I can tell that you're lying.

Tell me the places
you'd have me put my lips
and I'll tell you a hundred more.

You and I are incompatible chemicals.

We cannot mix.

We will explode.

&

She never finds him, you know.
Someone to watch over her.
He never comes.
And she knows he won't be coming.
That's why it sounds like an ache.

Blue and Killing Me Softly. Lauryn, not Roberta. That's your favorite color and your favorite song. And you like your eggs sunny side up and Shane from The Walking Dead and football, but not the Patriots.

I can tell you how I'll miss you if you can tell me how I like my eggs.

Every day is a struggle to pretend like I don't miss your hands. And that you didn't leave me for dead.

And now, I'm in love with Mickey's Bohemian Fingers. Me and Mickey's Bohemian Fingers go steady now. Me and Mickey's Bohemian Fingers fight dragons. Once, an evil witch put a spell on me with a poisoned apple and Mickey's Bohemian Fingers woke me by true love's kiss. Once, Lex Luthor pushed me off of a skyscraper and Mickey's Bohemian Fingers threw a cape on and caught me mid-air. Mickey's Bohemian Fingers and Kurt Cobain's fingers are arm wrestling for my honor as I write this. Also, the bartender at this joint has been giving me new ales to try for the last hour and they are *pre-heh-ty* fucking strong. But you totally can't tell, right?

⁖

When we were both lights, glowing and transcendent, you told the Makers that you wouldn't leave again unless They sent me with you. We were more than bodies then. More than any idea of love that either of us could fathom now. So they agreed to join us. Every time. And you promised that, no matter who or where I was, you'd find me. Every time.

You've kept your word.

You won't lose me if I'm not the body for you this whimper around. That's not how this works. We're not just skin. I'm something a little less temporary to you, and you know it. Something feels wrong when all is not right between us. We are well past coincidence. We were drawn. We were written. We are a cosmic game of hide and seek, you and I.

But today, she's your bride.

She's your bride, but I'm the boutonniere that never leaves your chest. I'm the smile for no reason when she begs you to tell her what you're so happy about. I'm the "something more" that tugs at you while you watch her searching through her purse for her lipstick. I'm the regret you'll never whisper to your granddaughter before you take your last breath.

You don't belong to me. I belong to *you*. You asked for me. Eons ago. And the universe said yes.

Hello again, darling. She looks lovely. And the pasta maker, that's from me.

So you've made it back to Cape Town and your sister and your oysters, and now I can't pass the color orange without thinking of you. We knew what it was when it was what it was, but I hope that you didn't drop my kiss off in the ocean on the way. For what it's worth, your curls have stayed in my pocket. Your laugh stays pinned to my jacket. Your fingers haven't left the back of my neck. I'll get over this. But I don't want you to until I do.

♦.

Of the millions of things that I need you for, to stand there and watch me burn is not one of them.

You didn't call when you said you would. [jab] I didn't pick up when you did. [block/cross/hook] You let your eyes stay just a little too long on that guy in the purple shirt. [cross/leg kick] I took him out on the dance floor. [spinning back-kick/mount] You wrote a post on Facebook about how you were "done with bi-polar little boys." [sweep/ground and pound] I clicked "Like". [sweep/clinch] You told me that you didn't want to battle anymore. [sweep/rear naked choke] I dropped my guard. I love you. [tap out]

1. If it is not you, it is...

a) someone better.
b) someone worse.
c) no one else.
d) none of the above.

2. If I fell for you, I can fall for...

a) someone else.
b) anyone.
c) no one else.
d) all of the above.

3. If I am not for you, I am for...

a) another.
b) no other.
c) you will always be for me.
d) none of the above.

4. If I was not yours, I would be...

a) someone else.
b) someone else's.
c) both (a) and (b).
d) but you are. mine.

"And you swear that you won't prick me?"
I asked.

"Cross my heart,"
the needle replied.

When I think about his penis,
it breaks my heart.
It was the most beautiful thing about him.

I stopped drinking hours before you did
just to see if I still loved your eyes.

Damn,
did
you
f
a
d
e
.
.
.

My favorite kind of kiss is the one where I'm on my back with my arms above my head, and he takes my wrists into his hands (either both wrists in one hand or one wrist per hand), and he centers his body between my legs (or straddles me, whichever) and he takes my mouth over with his.

My second favorite kind of kiss is a peck on the eyelids.

Your eyes are tiny universes that I love to get lost in, but it's hot as balls outside right now, so keep them pretty for me until sundown.

Lips like the thickest of honey and I want to feel them all over me...as soon as this plumber's done. No, I'm not leaving him with my key. Dude looks shady. My Macbook's here.

You are a knight in leather and cologne. I would follow you anywhere in the city, you have but to beckon. It's just that I bet Josh fifty bucks on this fight, so can you give me a couple of hours? Grab a table, I'll meet you there.

I want to make you roar my name to every heaven that's ever been called to...after my roommate leaves.

Yes, your voice is like strawberries and halos to me, but I can't just leave my mother waiting on the other line.

I bought a dozen roses, plucked the petals off by hand and sprinkled them on the floor for you to dance on. But I threw the stems in the garbage can and they're gonna start to stink in a few hours, and that's gonna kill everything, so lemme run this trash out real quick.

I have to tip the violin players I hired to play below your bedroom window. Hold that thought. Be right back.

I'm going to take your legs over my shoulders as soon as I get back from walking the dog.

My one, my sun,
my cinnamon plum,
do you need anything from the grocery store?

I'd love to sit on this phone and tell you every nasty, loving thing I want to do to your body, but my boss is on my ass because I came in late. I'm gonna bang the fuck out of you when my shift is over, though.

I love you more than love loves itself, but I have shit to do.

🍂.

UDGAF? IDGAF.
Like, WTFRU even...?

that time: in the shower.
you let me
shape your shampooed hair
into animals.
i made a duck.
we named it bernie.
bernie told you
to sing out loud
about how you loved the way
i felt in the steam.

here.

up

are

eyes

My

You've grown so tall.

10th grade?

Wow.

I'm so old.

You still into cars?

You were the only 11-year-old I knew

who could build a carburetor.

Yeah.

Yeah.

So.

I heard about the intervention.

I couldn't.

I just couldn't.

I hope your mom understood.

Did it work?

I'm sorry to hear that.

Yeah.

Yeah.

So.

But you look good!

Really grew into those dimples.

Don't slay all of the girls now.

Sometimes.

I think about him sometimes.

Not in the way I used to.

But, if he ever comes back, tell your brother I said hello and that there's no need to return my father's watch.

It's probably gone by now anyway.

I know, I know.

Thank you for trying.

I just hope that he's as happy with it as I am without him.

I'd love to call your mom sometime.

Maybe.

Sometime.

Yeah.

Yeah.

So.

It was good to see you too.

You'll always be my little brat.

You know that, right?

Yeah.

Yeah.

So.

I'll be seeing you.

Send your mom my love.

Take care of yourself.

⠂⠄ 🌑

I look down from your shaking gun to the red circle growing on the front of my shirt.

Things have been so weird between us lately.

You call me when you miss her. After the bars let out. You leave tears on my stomach. Tears on my bedsheets. Your socks balled up on my living room floor. My beer bottles, empty, on my kitchen counter. I send you out with a gentle squeeze on your neck. Pat you on the back. Like you're a friend. Like you're not a lover. You're not a friend. You're not a lover. This won't happen again. I won't pick up when you call. My phone's ringing.

He must be denim when you're in him
because you wear me like I'm silk.

I regret the way that we ended,
but I don't regret ever having met you.
It is pain that teaches us to love.
Life is but spark and memory.
How could we ever learn
to appreciate the truths
that blossom from the--?

Eh, fuck it.

I regret ever having met you.

There's something about his navel. Sometimes I think that my fingertips were made just to fit inside it. I rest my chin just beneath that navel and gaze up at him. His eyelids are seconds away from closing themselves into dreamland, but he's fighting it.

"There should probably be some words here, huh?" I say.

"Words like what?" His voice comes out in a hoarse whisper.

"Like poetry, sweet nothings."

"Can we skip it if I tip you?"

I press my thumb deep into the spot below his rib cage. He squirms. "Alright, alright," he gives.

"Now you *have* to say something."

He keeps his eyes on mine. I can see the wheels turning.

"The tics are tocking, babe," I say.

"Not fair," he says. "What do you say to someone who always leaves you speechless?"

I fold my lips into my mouth when I'm embarrassed and I know he knows this, so I lower my head and press my ear against that navel. He lays his hand on my head.

"Something like that, huh?" His final words before the sleep claims him for good.

An hour later, with my eyes still open and my head still glued to his stomach, I answer him.

"Yeah. Something like that."

take
me
with
you
left
me
here.

You knew I wouldn't believe you when you told me that you spoke Japanese. Show off.

Smirk.

And after I told you that hands were my favorite feature, you kept finding ways to call attention to yours. Bold. But it meant you were listening.

We talked on books and whales and fast cars and tarot cards. You believe in ghosts and I told you about poor Mr. Samuels forever haunting my old apartment, searching for his lost dog. You were surprised I'd seen *Daria*. Everybody's seen *Daria*.

Four in the morning and you didn't want to let me go. So tired we could barely keep our chins up, but we sat there in the cab of your truck, making sounds that sounded like stories. I let you wear my hat. I never let anyone wear my hat.

You made me promise to write you a poem on the next page, so turn it over.

Saturday night, Joseph had a drink.
Saturday night, Lisa went dancing.
Jimmy got laid.
Kat, Chris and Joe screamed
loud and long up at the moon.

For me,
there were no colored lights or music.

But my Sunday's got the better sun.

Saturday night, I had you.

"This is not love,"

said the mouse to the cat,

the grub to the bat,

the seed to the rat,

the fly to the frog,

the bird to the squall.

"This is not love.

No, it's not love at all."

⋮

"Will it hurt?"

"I don't know."

"Will you be there?"

"Where else would I be?"

"I'm cold."

"Come here."

"You promise you'll be there?"

"Where else would I be?"

I lost my virginity to a caveman on the back of an apatosaurus back when birds had scales and fish had feet.

That's how long I've been at this.

Baby, I've lit wicks for pirates and kings, chiefs and paupers. I was the reason that Burr shot Hamilton.

Been a man's trick, been his trade, been his trumpet, been his secret. An ingenue, an innocent. A blushing nymph. I'm as green as the color black. I built the block you've been around.

Bat those eyes, bite those lips. But when I say that I've met you before, I have. When I say that I've been here before, I have. And when I say that I want more now, I do.

Gangsters, princes, scholars, knights, the lot of them.

i'm not the lover you take to banquets or balls. i don't know how to wear a suit without squirming. i don't know the difference between a chardonnay and a merlot but you can bet puppies i've had too much of either. why couldn't i have worn my chucks with this tuxedo? these shiny shoes are killing my heels. i just used my gay powers to get your co-worker's wife to tell me what his penis looks like. she was pretty detailed. wanna know? i just talked the dj into playing "baby got back." i think it's time for these stiff upper lips to learn how to twerk. while your ceo is talking to us about golfing over this crème brûlée, my hand's beneath the table and between your legs. the bathroom attendant and i are hanging out tomorrow night. he says he knows a spot that does good karaoke. i'm in the corner challenging the servers to a pop-lock contest. foie gras is made out of *what*?! i love you. i might not be cut out for this, but you know that i love you. i just want to take this damn tie off. i just blew a kiss at the valet.

We have the same lips.
We tell the same lies.
We're Gemini twins,
if you squint your eyes.
The very same laugh.
The same shade of skin.
But he is not me,
and I am not him.

You're Paris,
London,
Yao,
León,
your lips of Minsk,
your eyes of Rome.

●.

I wish that I could roll your guilt into a fine cigar and smoke it over a steak and a glass of fine red. If I could just cash your guilt in like a paycheck, I'd fly my ass to Italy and take me a lover who might not be as smart as you, but he'd have big hands and a temper and he'd smell like sweet tobacco.

Here. Bring your guilt on over, so I can roll it into a ball and kick it across the yard. Bring it here, so I can grind it into seeds with my hands and sprinkle it on the ground for the pigeons and the crows. Let me steam it 'til it's milk and drink it 'til I'm full. Let me heat it up 'til it's twisted and black and hard like rock, so I can throw it through the window of that bitch-who-lives-across-the-street's house.

Yeah. Can your guilt fly? Can it bring me back a jewel from Sri Lanka? Can your guilt fertilize? Can it grow me my favorite tree? Can your guilt do these things for me?

Well, then keep it, love. Go 'head and keep it.

The night is just starting. I set my elbows on the edge of the club's table so that you see the curve of my back through my tight T-shirt. I keep my eyes on yours and then I look away. Some dude has a shirt that I admire. Or so I'd have you think. I pretend not to notice you walking over.

We're dancing now. Lips. Eyes. Lips. Eyes. Hips. Lips. Eyes. I stay close, hook my fingers into your waistband. You belong to me tonight. Your hands find their way to my chest. I let them stay there. Or I take them and trace them down my body until they can rest on the curve of my hips. Our foreheads brush. Only slightly. The tip of my nose finds your neck and I breathe in deeply. The double-shot of Petron works it's way through my blood. The music changes. Rihanna. I press my body against yours and take another sip of your drink.

We're at your place. Hot-talk and kisses. I run my fingers through your hair until I find the thickest spot and I grab on to it. My moans. One for the kiss on my neck. One for the brush of my nipples. One for your fingernails on my back. My hands try to grip your shoulder blades, but the sweat makes your back slippery, so I settle for your hips. My palm tightens around your ankle. We pop.

And again. My condom's gone, so we use one of yours. The comforter has fallen to the floor, but we don't notice. Your words run inconsistently and I giggle. We stain the mattress.

We're in your car. Outside of my apartment. An hour till day break. We made it just in time. I apologize for not being able to spend the night. "Work, you know." The usual lie. We touch lips and it's not nearly as uncomfortable to me as it is to you. You say something between a "thank you" and a "good bye". I smile. I lock the door before I shut it. It won't matter that I gave you the wrong number. You won't call it anyway. Some you marry, some you fuck.

When the sun rises and the juice wears off, I sit alone on my bed breathing in the Nag Champa. My skin smells like the body wash I used to clean you off of me. The TV runs.

I say my name out loud. And it sounds like a prayer. A wish. A hope. A curse. A vision. I wonder if you'll remember my name. I wonder if I'll remember yours. I wonder if you're doing the same thing that I am right now. I know the odds are that you're asleep. Somewhere, one of my faces thinks about the price I paid for a few hours of connection. I wonder how the story would have ended if I had met you in a coffee shop or a grocery store instead. I'm aware that I signed the contract. I agreed to play the game. Hell, I may have even created the rules. But being aware doesn't free me.

It might have been nice to know your middle name. Your favorite food. Your favorite color. It might have been nice to worry about your Valentine's Day gift. If your mother is going to like me. It might have been nice to tell you how much I loved you and meant it. I wonder what your voice would have sounded like saying the same words. I'll never know. Some you marry, some you fuck.

The night is just starting. I set my elbows just on the edge of the club's table so that you see the curve of my back through my tight T-shirt. I keep my eyes on yours, and then I look away. Some dude has a shirt that I admire. Or so I'd have you think. I pretend not to notice you walking over.

♣

Jen keeps textin' me.   Trynna see if I'm
alright.   Stop fuckin' textin' me, Jen.
    What does she think I'm gonna do? 'Been
crashin' on the couch.   Can't sleep in that
  bed.   That's the bed he used to
sleep with me in.   Fuck that bed.   I
should turn the TV on.   Play some
  Xbox.   I don't feel like playing Xbox.
    Almost down to my last   swallow.
    Gonna have to go to the liquor store for more.
          I don't wanna move.   I don't wanna
move right now.   I gotta text Jen back 'fore she
    sends the cops here. Six years.
Been with his ass for six years.   I can't drink
away six years in four days.   But I'll be
  damned if I ain't gon' try.   No.
    No.   I don't wanna forget him.   I
love him.   That's my baby. I love him.   I
    love   him, and he needs me.
    Despite all of the   bullshit, he
needs me.   I was by his side when he had no one
else.   He needs me.   Gonna clean myself
up.   Gonna get off of my ass.   I'm
comin'.   I'm comin' for you, baby.   Just
  gonna finish this drink.   Then I'm
gonna win him back.   I think I have a few
  dishes in the sink   that need to be washed.
    Fuck 'em.   Fuck the dishes and this
couch.   He's all in it.   Smells like him. I
    should probably change this shirt.
    Been wearin' this shirt since Sunday.
Since he left.   Stop texting me, Jen.   I
  need to shave.   I need to open a window.
    No.   I   don't want fresh air.   I
don't need to hear my neighbor's baby cryin'. I
don't want to lose his   smell.   Smells like
    him.   This ain't
  over.   He misses my lips.   He
                    misses my body.
    He needs me   around.   Just gonna
  finish this drink.   Then, I'm gonna
win him back.   Put on the red sneakers that

141

he bought me.   He didn't
ask for   them back.   And that
  cologne.   What was that cologne he
  liked?   I need to get some of that too.
     He left some books here. I can drop 'em off to
him.   Tell him I miss him.   Tell
him I can't be without him. What if she's at his
  place?   What if she's at his fuckin'
place when I show up?   I never would have
done that to him.   Six years, and his are the only
lips I've kissed.   I don't know what
she does that I didn't,   but I made
him scream.   I made his eyes roll.
     I let   him have all of it.   I know how
he likes it.   I   know how to touch him. I'm
 'a show her how to do him right.   And then,
  he's   gonna beg me to let him come back.
     He's gonna beg. Then, what's she gonna do?
         He misses me.   I know he's
     somewhere missing me.   All the
time we spent together?   It can't be
over like this.   Not like this.
Not like this, man.   I should play some Xbox.
                I don't feel like playing Xbox.
Just gonna finish this drink.   Then, I'm
             gonna win him back.

It's 'bout time,
'bout time
I took that boy
up off my head.

"M."
Christian St. Croix
San Diego, California
7 December 2015